A Life-Changing Proposition:
The $100M Offer Journey

Johnathan A. Barnes

TABLE OF CONTENTS

- Continuing the Pursuit of Growth and Success

Conclusion

INTRODUCTION

In the bustling metropolis of opportunity, where dreams collide with ambition, there lies an extraordinary tale of chance, courage, and destiny. "A Life-Changing Proposition: The $100M Offer Journey" unravels a captivating narrative that takes readers on an exhilarating expedition through the labyrinthine world of high-stakes business, life-altering choices, and personal transformation.

At its core, this book presents a unique convergence of real-life events and profound reflections on the power of a single proposition. In the midst of ordinary life, an extraordinary offer lands on the doorstep of our protagonist, forever altering the course of their existence. The lure of $100 million sets the stage for a captivating journey filled with exhilarating highs and crushing lows, leaving readers on the edge of their seats.

As the story unfolds, we delve deep into the inner workings of the human psyche, exploring the complexities of decision-making, ambition, and the quest for significance. Through the eyes of our protagonist, we witness the trials and tribulations of navigating the treacherous waters of wealth, power, and the price of success.

The book's narrative weaves together gripping anecdotes, intimate personal reflections, and powerful insights from influential figures who have encountered similar life-altering propositions. Through these diverse perspectives, readers gain invaluable wisdom, discovering that the journey to greatness is often paved with unforeseen challenges and transformative growth.

"A Life-Changing Proposition: The $100M Offer Journey" transcends mere financial aspirations; it serves as a metaphor for life's defining moments—those pivotal instances when destiny knocks, and the choices we make reverberate through time. The captivating storytelling and profound introspection invite readers to pause, contemplate, and examine their own lives. How would they respond if faced with an extraordinary proposition that could forever change the trajectory of their future?

As the pages turn, the book transcends the boundaries of a traditional narrative and transforms into a profound exploration of the human spirit the relentless pursuit of success, the fear of failure, and the resilience that arises from the deepest recesses of the soul. With each chapter, the emotional rollercoaster of triumph and turmoil deepens, forging a powerful connection between the readers and the characters, igniting a fire within to embrace the uncharted waters of their lives.

In a world where fortune favors the bold, "A Life-Changing Proposition: The $100M Offer Journey" is more than a gripping tale of financial pursuits it is a timeless testament to the boundless potential within each of us to face adversity, seize opportunities, and embrace the journey that shapes our destinies.

Embark on this life-changing expedition, for within the pages of this extraordinary tale lies the key to unlocking the hidden potential that lies dormant within us all.

CHAPTER 1

Embracing Life-Changing Opportunity

Life is a journey filled with unexpected twists and turns, presenting us with various opportunities that can transform our lives in profound ways. Embracing these life-changing opportunities requires courage, open-mindedness, and a willingness to step out of our comfort zones. Whether it's a career change, a chance to travel, or a leap of faith in personal growth, seizing these moments can lead to remarkable experiences and personal growth.

At the heart of embracing life-changing opportunities lies the concept of risk-taking. Stepping outside of our familiar routines and venturing into the unknown can be daunting, but it is precisely these risks that often hold the key to unlocking our true potential. When we open ourselves up to new possibilities, we allow ourselves to discover talents and strengths we may not have realized we possessed. Every opportunity, whether successful or not, offers valuable lessons and insights that contribute to our personal development.

One of the most common life-changing opportunities is career-related. Many individuals find themselves at crossroads in their professional lives, contemplating a shift into a new industry or pursuing an entrepreneurial venture. Embracing such opportunities demands self-belief, determination, and a vision for the future. By taking the leap, individuals not only enhance their skill sets but also experience personal fulfillment and a renewed sense of purpose.

Traveling, too, offers life-changing opportunities. Exploring new cultures, meeting diverse people, and experiencing unfamiliar landscapes can be transformative. Travel opens our minds to different perspectives, broadens our horizons, and fosters a sense of empathy and understanding for others. Whether it's a solo adventure or a group expedition, every journey shapes our outlook on life and leaves indelible memories.

Embracing life-changing opportunities may also involve taking a leap of faith in personal relationships. Love, in its many forms, can be a catalyst for transformative experiences. From starting a new relationship to reconciling with estranged family members, these opportunities to connect and heal can profoundly impact our emotional well-being and enrich our lives in ways we could never have imagined.

Overcoming fear and self-doubt are critical aspects of embracing life-changing opportunities. It is natural to feel hesitant when confronted with unfamiliar territory, but allowing fear to dictate our decisions can lead to missed chances and regrets. Instead, adopting a growth mindset and viewing challenges as opportunities for learning can empower us to take calculated risks and embrace life's offerings.

Embracing life-changing opportunities often involves a process of self-discovery. It requires introspection and a willingness to confront our desires, passions, and limitations. By understanding ourselves better, we gain clarity on the opportunities that align with our core values and aspirations. This self-awareness enables us to make informed decisions that resonate deeply with who we are and what we want from life.

Support from friends, family, or mentors can be invaluable when facing life-changing choices. Having a network of people who believe in us and encourage our growth can provide the necessary encouragement and reassurance during moments of uncertainty. These supportive relationships can also offer fresh perspectives and insights that aid in making informed choices.

Embracing life-changing opportunities is an ongoing process that requires adaptability and resilience. Not every opportunity may lead to the desired outcome, but each one contributes to our life's narrative. Embracing the journey, regardless of its twists and turns, enables us to live authentically, with a sense of purpose and gratitude for the diverse experiences that shape us.

Life is replete with opportunities that can transform us in profound ways. Embracing these life-changing moments requires courage, risk-taking, self-discovery, and support. Whether it's a career shift, travel adventure, or personal relationship, each opportunity offers the potential for growth and fulfillment. By opening ourselves up to new possibilities and facing challenges with determination and a growth mindset, we can embrace life-changing opportunities and create a life that reflects our true selves.

The Genesis of a Proposition

A proposition is the foundation of any argument, an idea or statement put forward for consideration. It is the seed from which persuasive debates, political policies, and societal changes spring. The genesis of a proposition is a fascinating journey, often shaped by human curiosity, critical thinking, and the need for progress. In this exploration, we will delve into the intricate process of how a proposition is born, nurtured, and eventually becomes a force to be reckoned with.

The genesis of a proposition starts with an inquisitive mind. Curiosity is the catalyst that sparks the initial thought, leading an individual to question the status quo or envision a new possibility. Whether it be a scientist seeking answers to unexplored phenomena, an activist advocating for social change, or an entrepreneur identifying an unmet need in the market, curiosity drives the inception of a proposition.

Once the seed of curiosity is planted, critical thinking comes into play. This stage involves thorough research, analysis, and reflection. Gathering data, studying existing literature, and examining historical precedents are all part of the process. It requires individuals to challenge assumptions, identify gaps in knowledge, and consider various perspectives before formulating a concrete proposition.

The process of refining a proposition often involves collaboration and constructive feedback. Engaging in discussions with peers, experts, and stakeholders helps to test the viability of the idea and strengthen its foundation. Embracing diverse viewpoints and open dialogue leads to well-rounded propositions that can withstand scrutiny and stand the test of time.

In politics, the genesis of a proposition often takes the form of a policy proposal. It emerges from the amalgamation of public opinion, expert advice, and the vision of a leader. Policy propositions are intended to address societal challenges, improve governance, and advance the common good. However, the journey from inception to implementation can be riddled with complexities, as political landscapes shift, and competing interests come into play.

In scientific research, propositions take the form of hypotheses. Scientists strive to unravel the mysteries of the universe by proposing educated guesses about natural phenomena. These propositions undergo rigorous testing through experiments and observations, ensuring that only the most robust theories survive and contribute to humanity's understanding of the world.

The genesis of a proposition also extends into the realm of innovation and entrepreneurship. Entrepreneurs identify gaps in the market, envision new products or services, and create propositions that have the potential to disrupt industries. The process of turning an idea into a successful business venture demands resilience, adaptability, and a relentless pursuit of excellence.

In social movements, propositions serve as the rallying cries for change. They emerge from the collective grievances of marginalized groups seeking justice, equality, and human rights. These propositions resonate with the hearts and minds of individuals, igniting passion and mobilizing communities to strive for a more inclusive and just society.

As a proposition gains traction, it faces challenges from opposing views, skepticism, and resistance to change. The ability to address these obstacles with well-reasoned arguments and evidence is essential for its success. Effective communication plays a vital role in persuading others to embrace the proposition's vision and contribute to its realization.

Over time, successful propositions can have a profound impact on society. They can shape public policies, transform industries, and change cultural norms. Think of the women's suffrage movement, the civil rights movement, or groundbreaking scientific discoveries each of these started as propositions and eventually reshaped the course of history.

The genesis of a proposition is a multifaceted and dynamic process. It begins with curiosity, thrives on critical thinking, and evolves through collaboration and resilience. Proposing ideas that challenge the status quo and inspire positive change is at the heart of human progress. As we continue to explore, innovate, and strive for a better world, the genesis of propositions will remain a fundamental part of our journey.

CHAPTER 2
Discovering the $100M Offer

In the bustling megalopolis of New York City, where dreams and intentions collide, a youthful entrepreneur named Alex set up himself at a crossroads. He'd spent times working on a tech incipiency, pouring his heart and soul into the adventure, but success sounded fugitive. Despite the multitudinous late nights and endless pitches, the advance he sought remained just out of reach. One cataclysmal autumn, as the sun dipped below the horizon, Alex entered an dispatch that would change his life ever. The subject line simply read," Once- in-a-lifetime occasion." Intrigued, he clicked on the communication and was saluted with a proposition that sounded too good to be true – a$ 100 million accession offer for his floundering incipiency. dubitation and excitement battled within him, but he knew he could not let this chance slip through his fritters.   As Alex excavated deeper into the mysterious dispatch, he discovered that the offer came from an enigmatic billionaire investor known only as"A. Winters." No information about this existent could be set up on the internet or through any traditional channels. Despite the query, Alex tasted that this might be his shot at turning his incipiency into a global success.   The dispatch requested a meeting at an exclusive extension suite in a luxurious   hostel. As he walked through the opulent lobby, he could not help but feel like he'd entered a scene from a Hollywood movie. Upon reaching the   extension, Alex was saluted by an perfectly dressed adjunct who steered him into a room adorned with priceless art and   stirring views of the megacity skyline. Winters sat behind a massive mahogany office, an air of riddle girding him. The discussion that followed was nothing short of surreal. The investor spoke in cryptic mysteries, revealing little about himself or his intentions. Still, he expressed an unvarying belief in Alex's implicit and the value of his incipiency. The billionaire emphasized that the$ 100 million offer was not just about plutocrat; it was a test of character, a trip of tone- discovery. Alex could not help but be   charmed by the enigmatic air ofA. Winters, feeling as though he'd stepped into a ultramodern- day puck tale. Despite the   appeal, the   youthful entrepreneur remained conservative. He sought advice from instructors and assiduity stagers, seeking to decrypt the true intentions behind the mysterious offer. Some prompted him to be cautious of implicit risks, while others encouraged him to take the vault of faith. As the days passed, Alex set up himself scuffling with a decision that transcended financial earnings. He questioned his bournes , the veritably substance of his dreams. Was he willing to relinquish control of his incipiency, the design that had defined him for so long, for the appeal of wealth and fame? In the midst of this internal struggle, Alex entered a sincere letter from an old friend and co-founder. It reminded him of the original spark that burned their entrepreneurial trip, the participated vision of changing the world with their groundbreaking technology. The letter stirred commodity deep within him, rejuvenating the passion that had fueled their incipiency from the veritably morning. With newfound clarity, Alex made his decision. He declined the$ 100 million offer, concluding to continue his incipiency's trip with his co-founder and the platoon they had erected together.A. Winters admired his choice, delivering him for staying true to his values and persuasions. As word of his decision spread, the media and tech world were aboil with admiration and conspiracy. Alex's story of turning down a life- changing sum of plutocrat for the sake of his vision inspired innumerous entrepreneurs worldwide. The$ 100 million offer had come a symbol of staying true to one's dreams, indeed in the face of unconceivable temptation. In the times that followed, Alex's incipiency flourished. It survived challenges, secured farther investments, and ultimately achieved the success he'd always pictured of. The decision to decline the offer had proven to be the right one, reaffirming the power of perseverance and staying true to one's persuasions. The mysteriousA. Winters continued to be an riddle, sometimes resurfacing in the media with whispers of other extravagant offers to youthful entrepreneurs. still, none of these stories captured the world's imagination relatively like Alex's trip. And so, the tale of discovering the$ 100 million offer came a ultramodern- day legend, inspiring innumerous romanticists and visionaries to follow their hearts and believe in the power of their dreams, no matter the cost. Alex's story served as a lamp of stopgap, reminding us all that the true worth of our dreams can not be measured in bare currency, but in the pursuit of passion and purpose.

The Visionaries Behind the Proposal

In every great endeavor, there are visionaries who dare to dream big and propose groundbreaking ideas that shape the course of history. Whether it's in the fields of science, technology, arts, or social change, these individuals possess an unwavering determination to push the boundaries of what is possible. The proposal at the center of this narrative is no exception, as it was born from the collaborative efforts of a remarkable group of visionaries whose brilliance and foresight continue to inspire and impact the world.

The genesis of the proposal can be traced back to a diverse team of experts from various disciplines, each contributing a unique perspective. Their shared passion for innovation and a better future brought them together, forging an alliance that would become the driving force behind the proposal's creation. Among these visionaries was Dr. Emily Parker, a brilliant scientist whose pioneering research in renewable energy set the stage for the ambitious project.

Dr. Parker's journey towards the proposal began during her early years in academia. Fascinated by the potential of sustainable energy sources, she dedicated herself to developing cutting-edge technologies that could revolutionize the world's energy landscape. Her tireless commitment to her research earned her international recognition and laid the groundwork for the grand proposal that would emerge years later.

Alongside Dr. Parker was Jack Ramirez, a visionary entrepreneur with a passion for transforming the way people interact with technology. Ramirez's success in the tech industry came from his ability to identify trends and anticipate the needs of consumers. With a deep understanding of the power technology holds in reshaping society, he sought to apply his expertise to the proposal, envisioning a future where technology and sustainability harmoniously coexisted.

As the team grew, so did their ambitions. Among the newest members was Elena Nguyen, an artist whose work transcended traditional mediums, pushing the boundaries of creativity and expression. Elena brought an artistic vision to the proposal, emphasizing the importance of creating an emotional connection between people and the project's goals. Her ability to blend aesthetics with functionality proved to be invaluable in shaping the proposal's public appeal.

However, the path to realization was far from smooth. The visionaries faced countless obstacles, from funding challenges to skepticism from established institutions. Yet, their shared conviction and determination kept them moving forward, undeterred by the naysayers. The turning point came when they secured the support of Dr. Samuel Brooks, a seasoned philanthropist with a track record of funding transformative projects. Dr. Brooks's belief in the visionaries' proposal injected the much-needed financial backing to bring their dream to life.

The proposal was a multidimensional initiative, tackling interconnected issues such as climate change, poverty, and education. It aimed to create a sustainable and inclusive future for generations to come. Central to the proposal was the construction of eco-friendly, smart cities, powered entirely by renewable energy. These cities would serve as models of innovation, incorporating cutting-edge technologies in transportation, urban planning, and resource management.

In addition to addressing environmental concerns, the visionaries also envisioned a comprehensive educational program that empowered individuals with the knowledge and skills needed to thrive in the evolving job market. This program was designed to bridge the digital divide and ensure equal opportunities for all, regardless of their background or location.

The proposal garnered significant attention, igniting discussions on the global stage. Political leaders, industry experts, and activists alike recognized the potential of the project to revolutionize societies and drive positive change on a global scale. As support for the proposal grew, so did the team's responsibilities. They found themselves leading a movement that called for collective action and a united commitment to building a better future.

In the face of skepticism and uncertainty, the visionaries' unwavering determination prevailed. The proposal became a reality, and the construction of the first sustainable smart city commenced. Its impact reached far beyond its physical boundaries, inspiring other communities and governments to adopt similar sustainable practices.

The visionaries behind the proposal continue to advocate for their vision, passionately sharing their insights and experiences to foster innovation and drive progress. Their legacy is not only the realization of a groundbreaking proposal but also the inspiration they instilled in future generations of dreamers and change-makers.

Navigating Uncertainty

In the world of business and negotiations, uncertainty is an ever-present companion, especially when it comes to high-stakes deals like a $100 million offer journey. Successfully navigating this uncertainty requires a strategic and adaptable approach, as well as a keen understanding of the factors at play.

The first step in handling uncertainty is conducting thorough research and due diligence. This involves gathering information about the target company, the market, competitors, and potential risks. A comprehensive understanding of the current economic landscape and industry trends is vital to make informed decisions during the negotiation process.

With research in hand, the next crucial aspect is building strong relationships and communication channels. Establishing trust and rapport with the parties involved can help ease tensions and encourage open discussions. Regular communication ensures that everyone is on the same page and allows for adjustments to be made as new information arises.

In a $100 million offer journey, timing is crucial. The market can change rapidly, and external factors like economic fluctuations or regulatory changes can influence the outcome of the deal. Adapting to these changes requires agility and quick decision-making. Being prepared for various scenarios and having contingency plans in place can provide a competitive advantage in the negotiation process.

Another essential factor is maintaining a long-term perspective. A $100 million deal is not only about immediate gains but also about the potential for future growth and profitability. Weighing short-term gains against long-term prospects helps in assessing the risks and rewards involved in the negotiation.

Uncertainty often leads to emotional responses, which can hinder the negotiation process. Emotional intelligence is vital in such situations to understand one's own emotions and the emotions of others involved in the deal. Managing emotions can prevent rash decisions and foster a more rational and productive negotiation environment.

Flexibility is a key attribute when navigating uncertainty. Rigidity can be detrimental to a successful deal, as unexpected challenges may require innovative solutions. Being open to creative alternatives and considering win-win outcomes can lead to a more constructive negotiation process.

Throughout the $100 million offer journey, it is essential to be mindful of the negotiation power dynamics. Understanding the relative strengths and weaknesses of each party allows for strategic positioning during the negotiation process. Maintaining leverage can enable better terms and conditions for the deal.

Moreover, seeking expert advice and guidance can be beneficial. Engaging skilled negotiators, legal advisors, and financial experts can provide valuable insights and increase the chances of a favorable outcome. These professionals bring their expertise to the table, assisting in making well-informed decisions amidst uncertainty.

Willingness to walk away from the deal is an important aspect to consider. Not all deals are worth pursuing, and sometimes it is better to avoid undue risks or unfavorable terms. Knowing when to step back can save time, resources, and potential regrets.

Navigating uncertainty in a $100 million offer journey requires a combination of strategic planning, effective communication, emotional intelligence, adaptability, and professional guidance. It is an intricate dance where decisions made and actions taken can significantly impact the final outcome. Embracing uncertainty as an inherent part of the negotiation process and leveraging it as an opportunity for growth can lead to successful deals and fruitful partnerships in the business world.

CHAPTER 3
Doubts and Second Thoughts

In the realm of business, opportunities often come with promises of great rewards, and sometimes, a once-in-a-lifetime offer can present itself in the form of a $100 million proposition. Such an immense amount can be life-changing, but with it also comes a flood of doubts and second thoughts that can cloud even the most resolute minds. In this essay, we explore the intricacies of such offers and the human psyche, delving into the factors that lead to doubts and the importance of discernment in making consequential decisions.

When confronted with an offer as significant as $100 million, one's initial reaction may be jubilation and excitement. The financial implications alone can create dreams of newfound wealth, security, and prosperity. However, as the initial euphoria subsides, doubts often begin to creep in, driven by a multitude of factors. Fear of the unknown, fear of failure, and the overwhelming pressure of making a pivotal decision all contribute to this internal conflict.

Second thoughts may also stem from the hesitancy to leave behind familiar surroundings, such as a well-established career or a close-knit community. The thought of venturing into uncharted territories can be both exhilarating and terrifying, as it challenges one's sense of identity and comfort zone. Additionally, the weight of responsibility that comes with managing such a colossal sum of money can be daunting, leading to doubts about one's ability to handle the newfound wealth wisely.

Another critical factor that plays a role in fostering doubts is the influence of external opinions. When faced with a life-changing decision, seeking advice from friends, family, or business associates is natural. However, this external input can often cloud one's judgment and lead to further confusion. The pressure to conform to others' expectations or to please everyone can stifle individual discernment, making it challenging to distinguish between constructive advice and undue influence.

In contrast, embracing doubts and second thoughts can be a valuable process of introspection. It allows individuals to explore the full spectrum of possibilities, contemplate potential pitfalls, and assess the alignment of the offer with their personal values and long-term goals. Doubts serve as a natural defense mechanism, prompting a deeper evaluation of the consequences, risks, and potential rewards, ultimately leading to more informed decisions.

Deciphering whether the doubts are the result of genuine concerns or mere anxieties becomes crucial in such circumstances. Engaging in thorough due diligence, seeking professional advice from experts in relevant fields, and analyzing the offer from multiple perspectives can help address these concerns and build a clearer picture of the situation. Emphasizing a balanced approach to decision-making can help mitigate unnecessary doubts and make the process less overwhelming.

Acknowledging that doubts are a part of the human experience and embracing them as an integral aspect of growth and self-awareness can empower individuals to make more confident choices. Rather than viewing doubts as a sign of weakness, they can be seen as an opportunity to deepen one's understanding of oneself and the external world.

It is crucial to recognize that the decision to accept or decline a $100 million offer is highly subjective and dependent on individual circumstances. There is no one-size-fits-all solution. The path chosen may not be the same for everyone, and that is entirely acceptable.

Doubts and second thoughts are natural companions of life-altering decisions, such as a $100 million offer. The magnitude of such an offer can evoke a range of emotions, from excitement to apprehension. Understanding the underlying factors contributing to doubts, embracing them as part of the decision-making process, and seeking clarity through comprehensive analysis are essential steps in making an informed choice. Ultimately, regardless of the decision made, what remains paramount is an individual's pursuit of personal growth, fulfillment, and happiness.

Preparing for Transformation

Transformation is an inherent part of life. Just as seasons change and caterpillars turn into butterflies, individuals and organizations must undergo their own metamorphoses to adapt, thrive, and progress. Embracing change and preparing for transformation is not merely an option; it is a necessity in a rapidly evolving world.

The first step in preparing for transformation is recognizing the need for change. Whether it is a personal realization or an organization's acknowledgment of market shifts, identifying the factors that necessitate transformation is crucial. Denial or resistance to change can hinder progress and lead to stagnation. Instead, accepting the inevitability of change sets the stage for a proactive approach.

Next, one must cultivate a growth mindset. Viewing challenges as opportunities for learning and improvement allows individuals and organizations to remain flexible in the face of transformation. A growth mindset encourages experimentation, innovation, and a willingness to take calculated risks, fostering resilience and adaptability.

To facilitate transformation, proper planning and strategizing are essential. Setting clear goals and objectives provides a roadmap for the journey ahead. Moreover, establishing a timeline and identifying milestones helps measure progress and maintain focus. Flexibility within the plan is equally crucial, as unexpected hurdles are inevitable. Agile planning enables adjustments and ensures the transformation stays on track.

Communication plays a pivotal role in preparing for transformation, particularly in organizational settings. Transparent and open communication with stakeholders fosters understanding, garnering support, and reducing anxiety during times of change. Leaders who effectively communicate the vision and reasons behind transformation create a shared sense of purpose, motivating teams to embrace the upcoming challenges.

Another vital aspect of preparing for transformation is investing in skills development and knowledge acquisition. Individuals and organizations must equip themselves with the necessary tools and expertise to navigate the changing landscape. Training programs, workshops, and continuous learning initiatives not only enhance capabilities but also promote a culture of growth and adaptability.

Embracing a culture of experimentation and tolerance for failure can foster innovation and creative problem solving. Encouraging employees to test new ideas and learn from mistakes instills a sense of ownership and empowerment. This mindset shift is crucial in preparing individuals and organizations for transformation, as it promotes a proactive approach towards change.

In preparing for transformation, it is essential to address potential roadblocks and challenges that may arise. Resistance to change, fear of the unknown, and complacency are common hurdles that can hinder progress. Identifying and addressing these obstacles early on allows for proactive strategies to mitigate their impact.

Seeking inspiration from success stories of transformation can provide valuable insights and motivation. Learning from others who have undergone successful transformations can illuminate potential pitfalls and best practices. These examples can serve as beacons of hope and determination, reinforcing the belief that transformation is both achievable and worthwhile.

Celebrating progress and milestones along the transformation journey is vital. Acknowledging achievements and expressing gratitude to those involved fosters a positive atmosphere, encouraging continued commitment and effort. Recognizing and rewarding perseverance reinforces the value of transformation and its positive impact.

Preparing for transformation is not a one-time task; it is an ongoing journey of growth and adaptation. By embracing change, nurturing a growth mindset, planning strategically, communicating effectively, investing in skills development, and fostering a culture of experimentation, individuals and organizations can position themselves for successful transformation. Through perseverance, determination, and a collective effort, transformation becomes an opportunity for positive change and a stepping stone towards a brighter future.

CHAPTER 4
Cultivating the Right Mindset

The mortal mind is a important tool that can either be a great supporter or a redoubtable handicap on the path to particular growth and success. The conception of cultivating the right mindset revolves around developing a positive, flexible, and growth- acquainted approach to life. In this essay, we will explore how cultivating the right mindset workshop and its impact on colorful aspects of one's life. A mindset is a set of beliefs, stations, and studies that shape how we perceive and respond to the world around us. The first step in cultivating the right mindset is tone- mindfulness. This involves examining our studies and feting any negative or limiting beliefs that may be holding us back. formerly apprehensive, we can begin to challenge these beliefs and replace them with further empowering bone . One of the abecedarian aspects of the right mindset is espousing a growth mindset. Chased by psychologist Carol Dweck, a growth mindset is the belief that one's capacities and intelligence can be developed through trouble, perseverance, and literacy. Embracing a growth mindset allows individualities to view challenges as openings for growth rather than as invincible obstacles. This perspective fosters adaptability, perseverance, and a amenability to take on new challenges. Another pivotal element in cultivating the right mindset is maintaining a positive station. A positive mindset not only improves our overall well- being but also influences how we handle lapses and failures. Rather than dwelling on negativity, a positive mindset helps us concentrate on results, leading to further effective problem working and decision timber. Cultivating the right mindset involves setting clear pretensions and developing a sense of purpose. Setting specific, attainable pretensions gives direction to our sweats and provides provocation to keep moving forward. Having a sense of purpose gives our conduct lesser meaning and helps us stay married to our bournes . To cultivate the right mindset, it's essential to exercise tone- compassion and grasp failure as a stepping gravestone to success. Admitting that failure is a natural part of the literacy process allows us to be more forgiving of ourselves and maintain our tone- regard. By learning from failures and using them as openings for growth, we develop a sense of adaptability that propels us toward success. girding ourselves with positive and probative individualities plays a significant part in cultivating the right mindset. The people we associate with influence our stations and beliefs. Being in the company of like inclined individualities who encourage and support our growth can enhance our determination and inspire us to reach our full eventuality. awareness and contemplation also play a pivotal part in cultivating the right mindset. These practices help individualities come more present and apprehensive of their studies and feelings. By rehearsing awareness, we can more control our responses, reduce stress, and make further conscious choices aligned with our pretensions. Cultivating the right mindset doesn't be overnight; it requires harmonious trouble and practice. One effective system is to produce diurnal rituals and positive habits that support the asked mindset. These may include reading inspiring books, journaling, or engaging in positive declarations. The impact of cultivating the right mindset extends beyond individual growth; it influences how we interact with others and approach challenges in colorful areas of life. In the professional sphere, a growth mindset fosters invention and rigidity, allowing individualities and associations to thrive in an ever-changing world. In connections, a positive mindset can ameliorate communication and foster empathy and understanding. Cultivating the right mindset can appreciatively affect internal and physical health. Reducing stress and anxiety through a positive outlook can lead to better overall well- being and adaptability against ails. Studies have shown that individualities with a growth mindset tend to have lower situations of cortisol, the stress hormone, which further demonstrates the significance of mindset in health issues. Cultivating the right mindset is a transformative trip that empowers individualities to unleash their full eventuality and grasp life's challenges with sanguinity and adaptability. Through tone- mindfulness, espousing a growth mindset, maintaining positivity, setting pretensions, and rehearsing tone compassion, individualities can develop a mindset that propels them towards particular growth and success in all areas of life. By nurturing this mindset and making it a part of diurnal life, we pave the way for a more fulfilling and poignant actuality, not only for ourselves but also for those around us.

A Journey of Negotiation

In the intricate dance of human interaction, negotiation stands as an essential skill. Whether in personal relationships, business deals, or diplomatic endeavors, the art of negotiation shapes outcomes, fosters compromise, and drives progress. Like an unfolding story, a journey of negotiation weaves through challenges, emotions, and strategies, ultimately leading to the destination of agreement.

Setting the Stage:

Every negotiation begins with a context a backdrop that shapes the participants' intentions and objectives. It could be two business partners seeking to finalize a merger, diplomats negotiating peace treaties, or even a couple discussing their future together. Understanding the underlying interests and motivations of all parties involved lays the foundation for a successful negotiation.

Building Relationships:

Relationships play a pivotal role in negotiations. Trust and rapport create an environment where ideas can flow freely, and participants can explore creative solutions. Establishing a human connection helps dissolve barriers, enabling individuals to see each other as collaborators rather than adversaries.

Identifying Interests:

Beyond the surface positions taken by negotiators lie their underlying interests. Unearthing these interests allows negotiators to discover common ground and explore mutually beneficial solutions. Often, interests differ from stated positions, and delving into these nuances is essential for a fruitful negotiation.

Art of Communication:

Clear and effective communication is the backbone of any negotiation. Active listening, precise articulation, and the ability to empathize with the other party's perspective foster understanding and respect. Miscommunications and misunderstandings can lead negotiations astray, so constant vigilance in communication is vital.

Maneuvering Through Obstacles:

A journey of negotiation is rarely smooth sailing. Obstacles arise in the form of conflicts, disagreements, and resistance to change. Skillful negotiators navigate these challenges adeptly, focusing on win-win solutions that address concerns while achieving mutual objectives.

The Power Dynamic:

Power imbalances often influence the negotiation process. One party may possess more leverage or control over resources, tilting the scales in their favor. Understanding the power dynamics and addressing them fairly helps prevent exploitation and builds a more equitable negotiation environment.

Cultural Nuances:

In a globalized world, negotiations often involve individuals from diverse cultural backgrounds. Being aware of cultural nuances, customs, and communication styles is crucial to avoiding misunderstandings and fostering cross-cultural collaboration.

Emotions in the Mix:

Emotions play a profound role in negotiations. From excitement and hope to frustration and disappointment, a range of feelings can influence the negotiation process. Skilled negotiators manage emotions constructively, recognizing when emotions are affecting decision-making and finding ways to refocus on the issues at hand.

Unraveling Deadlocks:

Deadlocks and impasses are common in complex negotiations. At such junctures, creative problem-solving and alternative solutions become imperative. Mediators or third-party facilitators may also step in to help break the stalemate and guide negotiators towards resolution.

Embracing Win-Win Outcomes:

The most successful negotiations lead to win-win outcomes, where both parties feel satisfied with the agreement. These agreements are more sustainable and lay the groundwork for future collaborations and positive relationships.

The Art of Closure:

As the journey of negotiation draws to a close, the final agreement must be documented and sealed. Ensuring clear and unambiguous terms protects the interests of both parties and helps avoid future disputes.

Reflecting on the Journey:

A thoughtful negotiation doesn't end with the agreement; it involves reflection on the process itself. Analyzing successes and learning from challenges enhances negotiators' skills, empowering them for future negotiations.

A journey of negotiation involves understanding, empathy, communication, and creative problem-solving. It weaves through complexities and emotions, ultimately paving the way for agreements that serve the interests of all parties involved. With each negotiation, individuals evolve as negotiators, enriching their abilities to shape a world where collaboration triumphs over conflicts.

CHAPTER 5

Thriving in High-Stakes Negotiations

High-stakes negotiations are intense, high-pressure situations that can make or break critical business or even international agreements. Thriving in such scenarios requires a combination of strategic thinking, effective communication, emotional intelligence, and adaptability. In this article, we will explore the key principles and strategies that can help individuals and teams succeed in high-stakes negotiations, ultimately achieving favorable outcomes and maintaining valuable relationships.

Understanding the Landscape :

To thrive in high-stakes negotiations, one must first understand the landscape. This involves conducting thorough research on the parties involved, their interests, strengths, and weaknesses. Identifying potential alternatives and fallback options can provide leverage during the negotiation process. Additionally, understanding cultural norms and communication styles can help build rapport and avoid misunderstandings.

Cultivating Emotional Intelligence :

Emotional intelligence plays a crucial role in high-stakes negotiations. Remaining composed and managing emotions under pressure is essential to making sound decisions. Active listening and empathy can foster trust and build rapport with the other parties involved, paving the way for more constructive dialogue. Recognizing and addressing one's own biases can also prevent irrational judgments that may hinder the negotiation process.

Setting Clear Objectives :

Clearly defining objectives is paramount in high-stakes negotiations. Establishing specific, measurable, achievable, relevant, and time-bound (SMART) goals provides a clear direction and prevents getting sidetracked during the discussions. Keeping these objectives at the forefront helps maintain focus and prevents unnecessary concessions that may jeopardize the desired outcomes.

Building a Strong Team :

A successful high-stakes negotiation often involves a team effort. Assembling a diverse team with complementary skills and perspectives can enhance problem-solving capabilities and strategic planning. Assigning specific roles and responsibilities ensures a coordinated approach, maximizing the team's effectiveness. Regular communication and collaboration within the team are vital to maintaining unity and adaptability during the negotiation process.

Effective Communication :

Clear and effective communication is the backbone of high-stakes negotiations. Expressing thoughts concisely, persuasively, and respectfully can sway the other party's opinions. Active listening and asking thoughtful questions demonstrate genuine interest and encourage reciprocity. Non-verbal cues, such as body language and tone of voice, also contribute to the overall message conveyed. Regular updates and feedback within the negotiation team can aid in adjusting strategies as needed.

Negotiation Strategies :

Various negotiation strategies can be employed in high-stakes situations. Principled negotiation, based on mutual interests and collaborative problem-solving, can foster win-win outcomes. However, knowing when to employ assertiveness and competitive tactics can be equally important. Balancing assertiveness and cooperation can demonstrate strength while preserving relationships. Flexibility and adaptability in the face of unforeseen challenges can be crucial in maintaining a strong negotiating position.

Managing Pressure and Deadlines :

High-stakes negotiations often come with tight deadlines and intense pressure. Thriving in such situations involves effective time management, prioritization, and keeping a cool head under pressure. Allocating time wisely for preparation, discussions, and decision-making can prevent rash decisions. Leveraging deadlines strategically can motivate the other party to act and make concessions.

Thriving in high-stakes negotiations demands a blend of preparation, emotional intelligence, communication skills, and strategic acumen. By understanding the landscape, setting clear objectives, cultivating strong teams, and employing effective negotiation strategies, individuals and teams can navigate these intense situations successfully, securing favorable outcomes and nurturing valuable relationships.

Overcoming Obstacles and Challenges

Life is a trip filled with ups and campo, and along the way, we encounter colorful obstacles and challenges that test our strength, adaptability, and determination. These hurdles can come in colorful forms, similar as particular struggles, professional lapses, health issues, or societal pressures. still, it's in prostrating these obstacles that we learn and grow, shaping the veritably substance of who we're as individualities. Facing obstacles is an essential part of the mortal experience. Each person's trip is unique, and so are the challenges they encounter. Some may face fiscal rigors, while others grapple with tone mistrustfulness and precariousness. Anyhow of the nature of the handicap, the key lies in admitting its presence and embracing it as an occasion for growth. One of the first way in prostrating challenges is developing a positive mindset. It's easy to succumb to negativity when facing obstacles, but espousing a positive outlook can empower us to find creative results. By shifting our focus from the problem itself to implicit results, we open ourselves up to new possibilities and perspectives. Seeking support from others can make a significant difference in navigating through challenges. Whether it's family, musketeers, instructors, or support groups, participating our struggles with others can give precious perceptivity, stimulant, and emotional support. Flash back, you do not have to face challenges alone. Adaptability is another crucial factor in prostrating obstacles. Life's challenges may knock us down, but it's our capability to bounce back and persist that defines us. Adaptability involves conforming to change, learning from failures, and noway giving up on our pretensions, no matter how delicate the trip becomes. Along the path to success, lapses and failures are ineluctable. They serve as important preceptors, guiding us to upgrade our strategies and come more set for the future. Thomas Edison famously said," I haven't failed. I have just set up 10,000 ways that will not work" when contriving the light bulb. Embracing failures as stepping monuments towards success can transfigure obstacles into openings. In addition to particular challenges, societal pressures and prospects can weigh heavily on an existent's path. Breaking free from societal morals and embracing one's true tone can be a daunting task. still, it's pivotal to flash back that the utmost fulfilling life is one lived genuinely, staying true to one's values and heartstrings, anyhow of external influences. The biggest handicap is the fear of the unknown. Stepping out of our comfort zones and taking pitfalls can be intimidating, but it's frequently where the most profound growth occurs. Embracing query and believing in our capacities can lead to remarkable metamorphoses. prostrating obstacles also involves embracing change. Life is ever- changing, and defying it can produce gratuitous walls. By being flexible and adaptable, we can navigate transitions more easily and be more set for the challenges that lie ahead. likewise, tolerance and perseverance are essential merits in the face of adversity. prostrating obstacles infrequently happens overnight. It requires harmonious trouble, fidelity, and the amenability to stay the course, indeed when progress seems slow. Trusting the process and being patient with oneself are vital rudiments of the trip. prostrating obstacles and challenges is an integral part of the mortal experience. It's through these struggles that we discover our inner strength, adaptability, and implicit for growth. By espousing a positive mindset, seeking support, remaining flexible, learning from failures, embracing change, and staying true to ourselves, we can navigate the obstacles on our path to success. Flash back, the trip may be laborious, but it's in prostrating these challenges that we find the true meaning and fulfillment in our lives. So, face the obstacles head- on, for they're stepping monuments to a brighter and stronger future.

CHAPTER 6

Leaving Comfort Zones Behind

In the realm of business and entrepreneurship, many trials allure the imagination as much as the pursuit of a$ 100 million offer. This audacious thing pushes individualities to explore uncharted homes, grasp query, and leave their comfort zones before. Embarking on such a trip requires a unique mix of courage, adaptability, and rigidity. Let us claw into the transformative process of how leaving comfort zones behind workshop in the pursuit of a$ 100 million offer. Embracing the strange Leaving comfort zones begins with a amenability to embrace the strange. Entrepreneurs seeking a$ 100 million offer frequently venture into unexplored requests, diligence, or disruptive technologies. It requires the capability to set aside preconceived sundries and open bone 's mind to new possibilities. Taking Calculated pitfalls Bold bournes frequently come with great pitfalls. still, successful individualities in the$ 100 million offer trip understand the value of taking advised pitfalls. threat assessment, strategic planning, and contingency measures are essential factors of decision- making in the pursuit of such an ambitious thing. Fostering a Growth Mindset A growth mindset is a pivotal asset when leaving comfort zones. This mindset embraces challenges, sees failures as learning openings, and continually seeks tone- enhancement. Entrepreneurs seeking for a $100million offer constantly seek knowledge, feedback, and mentorship to upgrade their strategies. prostrating Fear of Failure The fear of failure can be paralyzing, especially when trying commodity extraordinary. Successful individualities in the$ 100 million offer trip admit the fear but choose to face it head- on. They fete that failure isn't a destination but a stepping gravestone toward success. erecting a Strong Support System Leaving comfort zones before isn't a solitary pursuit. It requires a strong support system, including instructors, counsels, mates, and a platoon of devoted individualities. This network provides stimulant, guidance, and the necessary moxie to navigate uncharted waters successfully. Embracing nonstop adaption The business geography is dynamic, and unlooked-for challenges are ineluctable. Those aiming for a$ 100 million offer must be willing to acclimatize continually. Inflexibility in strategy and a amenability to pivot when demanded are pivotal to staying ahead in the ever- changing request. Adaptability in the Face of lapses lapses are an essential part of any significant trip. Entrepreneurs aiming for a$ 100 million offer must develop adaptability to brio back from failures and bummers. Adaptability enables them to stay focused on the end thing, indeed during the darkest moments. Staying Committed to the Vision Maintaining unvarying commitment to the vision of a$ 100 million offer is vital. This commitment energies determination, sustains provocation, and inspires the entire platoon to push beyond their limits. Leaders must continually remind themselves and their platoon of the vision to keep everyone aligned.

Celebrating mileposts While the $ 100 million offer may be the ultimate destination, celebrating mileposts along the way is essential. Admitting progress and achievements boosts morale, fosters a positive atmosphere, andre-energizes the platoon for the trip ahead. Learning from Failure and Success Reflection is a important tool for growth. Entrepreneurs on the path to a $ 100 million offer learn from both their failures and successes. assaying past gests enables them to fine- tune their strategies, subsidize on strengths, and alleviate sins. In conclusion, the trip of pursuing a$ 100 million offer is a transformative experience that demands leaving comfort zones before. Embracing the strange, taking advised pitfalls, fostering a growth mindset, prostrating fear, and erecting a strong support system are pivotal way. The capability to acclimatize, adaptability in the face of lapses, commitment to the vision, celebrating mileposts, and learning from gests each contribute to the ultimate consummation of this audacious thing. Only those willing to push beyond boundaries, both tête-à-tête and professionally, can truly grasp the openings that lie beyond their comfort zones and achieve the extraordinary.

Adapting to New Realities

Adapting to new realities is a fundamental aspect of human existence. Throughout history, individuals, societies, and civilizations have faced an ever-changing world, requiring constant adjustments and innovations.

In the modern era, this adaptability has become even more critical as rapid technological advancements, globalization, and unforeseen challenges constantly reshape our lives.

At the core of adapting to new realities lies the human capacity for resilience. When confronted with unexpected circumstances, individuals must exhibit flexibility, open-mindedness, and a willingness to learn and evolve. Whether it's coping with personal challenges, embracing technological advancements, or navigating societal transformations, the process of adaptation requires a multidimensional approach.

One key aspect of adapting to new realities is recognizing the need for change. Accepting that the status quo may no longer be sustainable or appropriate is the first step towards growth. It involves acknowledging potential limitations, understanding the reasons behind the necessity for change, and overcoming the fear of uncertainty. Adapting to new realities often means letting go of familiar routines and embracing the unknown.

In the face of change, embracing a growth mindset becomes crucial. This mindset emphasizes the belief that abilities and intelligence can be developed through dedication and hard work. By adopting a growth mindset, individuals become more willing to take on new challenges, learn from failures, and continuously improve. Instead of viewing change as a threat, they perceive it as an opportunity for personal and professional development.

Additionally, staying informed and remaining adaptable in the face of new information is essential. The world is in a constant state of flux, and being receptive to new knowledge and perspectives is key to adapting successfully. Learning from different sources, engaging in meaningful conversations, and seeking diverse viewpoints enrich one's understanding and capacity to adapt.

Another vital aspect of adapting to new realities is fostering a culture of innovation and creativity. Encouraging experimentation, valuing diverse perspectives, and creating an environment that embraces change enable organizations and communities to thrive in dynamic landscapes. The ability to adapt is not solely an individual trait; it also requires collective efforts and collaborative problem-solving.

In times of significant change, resilience serves as a powerful tool. Resilience allows individuals and communities to bounce back from adversity, learn from setbacks, and find new ways to thrive. Building resilience involves developing coping strategies, cultivating social support networks, and nurturing emotional well-being.

Technology plays a crucial role in facilitating adaptation to new realities. The rapid advancement of technology has reshaped industries, economies, and societies. Embracing technological innovations and digital transformation becomes essential for staying relevant and competitive in the modern world. Technology also provides tools and platforms for connecting, collaborating, and disseminating knowledge, enhancing the adaptability of individuals and organizations alike.

However, while adapting to new realities is vital, it is equally crucial to strike a balance between embracing change and preserving essential aspects of our identity and values. Change should not lead to the erasure of cultural heritage, ethical principles, or the natural world. Instead, adaptation should be guided by a mindful approach that considers the broader impact on individuals and the planet.

Adapting to new realities is a multifaceted process that requires individuals and societies to exhibit resilience, embrace change, and foster a growth mindset. Staying informed, remaining open to new knowledge, and fostering a culture of innovation are essential components of successful adaptation. Moreover, technology plays a critical role in enabling individuals and organizations to navigate change effectively. Throughout history, humanity has demonstrated its capacity to adapt, and in the face of future challenges, the ability to embrace change will continue to be the driving force behind progress and human development.

CHAPTER 7

Impact on Personal Relationships

Life-changing propositions have the potential to profoundly impact personal relationships. When faced with pivotal decisions that alter the trajectory of one's life, relationships with family, friends, and romantic partners can undergo significant transformations. These propositions can be anything from relocating to a new city, pursuing a different career, ending or beginning a serious commitment, or embarking on a personal development journey. The consequences of these choices ripple through the fabric of our lives and the connections we hold dear.

One of the most apparent effects of life-changing propositions on personal relationships is the potential for distance or separation. For instance, when one decides to move away for educational or career opportunities, it can strain relationships with loved ones left behind. Long-distance friendships and romantic partnerships require extra effort to maintain and can lead to feelings of loneliness and isolation.

On the flip side, life-changing propositions can also serve as catalysts for deepening bonds. Sharing transformative experiences with others can forge stronger connections, creating a sense of unity and mutual growth. When individuals in a relationship embark on personal development journeys together, they may become more empathetic and supportive of each other's growth, leading to a more profound and fulfilling connection.

Life-changing propositions can unveil hidden aspects of ourselves and our loved ones. Facing challenges, stepping outside comfort zones, or dealing with unexpected outcomes can reveal resilience and strengths we didn't know we possessed. Similarly, we might discover unexpected aspects of those close to us, leading to newfound admiration or understanding.

It's important to acknowledge that not all relationships survive life-changing propositions. Some may wither under the weight of differing goals, values, or priorities that emerge as a result of the proposed changes. In such cases, individuals may drift apart, leading to feelings of loss and grief. It's essential to recognize that as life evolves, so too can our connections, and letting go can be an act of growth and self-care.

Communication plays a critical role in navigating the impact of life-changing propositions on relationships. Open and honest conversations about intentions, fears, and expectations can foster understanding and support. Additionally, active listening and empathy help create an environment where all parties feel heard and respected, paving the way for healthy and evolving relationships.

The way we perceive and approach life-changing propositions can also influence their impact on personal relationships. Embracing a growth mindset and viewing challenges as opportunities for development can facilitate resilience and adaptability in relationships. Conversely, fixed mindsets that resist change may impede the evolution of connections and hinder personal growth.

Life-changing propositions can shed light on the balance between individual and collective needs within relationships. It is essential to strike a healthy equilibrium between personal aspirations and the shared goals of the relationship. Sometimes, compromises need to be made, while other times, partnerships may evolve to better support each other's individual paths.

Handling the impact on personal relationships in life-changing propositions requires a level of self-awareness. Understanding one's motivations and priorities enables individuals to make informed decisions that align with their values and life goals. This self-awareness can also extend to understanding the needs and desires of those they are in relationships with, fostering mutual respect and consideration.

Life-changing propositions have far-reaching effects on personal relationships. They can lead to both distance and connection, unveiling hidden depths within ourselves and our loved ones. Some relationships may thrive, while others may falter, and in certain cases, letting go can be an act of growth. Communication, empathy, and a growth mindset are essential tools in navigating the impact of these propositions on our relationships. Ultimately, embracing self-awareness and striking a balance between personal aspirations and collective goals can pave the way for stronger, more fulfilling connections as life unfolds.

Lessons from the $100M Offer Journey

In the trip of entering a$ 100 million offer, there are inestimable assignments to be learned that extend beyond the financial value of the deal. Such an experience provides perceptivity into entrepreneurship, decision- timber, concession, and particular growth. Let's claw into the assignments from this extraordinary trip.

Assignment 1 Vision and continuity entering a$ 100 million offer does not be overnight. It starts with a strong vision and unwavering continuity. Successful entrepreneurs frequently have a clear thing and are determined to overcome obstacles along the way, making offerings and staying concentrated on their objects.

Assignment 2 Rigidity Inflexibility is pivotal in the fast-paced world of business. The trip to a$ 100 million offer requires entrepreneurs to acclimatize their strategies, pivot when necessary, and stay ahead of request trends. Being open to change can lead to unanticipated openings and success.

Assignment 3 Surround Yourself with the Right platoon Behind every successful entrepreneur is a able platoon. erecting a professed, different, and cohesive platoon is essential for diving challenges and seizing openings. Having the right people by your side can make all the difference in achieving remarkable results.

Assignment 4 Calculated pitfalls Entrepreneurship involves taking pitfalls, but not all pitfalls are created equal. A $100 million offer trip calls for calculated pitfalls that align with the business's vision and eventuality for growth. Understanding threat- price rates is pivotal for making strategic opinions. Assignment 5 Valuing Innovation Innovation is the lifeblood of a thriving business. Embracing invention, whether through groundbreaking technology, unique product immolations, or disruptive business models, is crucial to staying competitive and attracting implicit investors or acquirers.

Assignment 6 erecting a Strong Brand A strong brand identity is a important asset. It differentiates a company from its challengers, builds trust with guests, and attracts implicit investors. harmonious branding across all aspects of the business can significantly enhance its value.

Assignment 7 client Centric Approach Putting the client at the center of everything is essential for long- term success. Understanding client requirements, gathering feedback, and continuously perfecting products or services can lead to pious guests and a advanced valuation.

Assignment 8 concession Chops entering a $ 100 million offer involves negotiating with implicit buyers or investors. Having strong concession chops, including the capability to communicate effectively, understand the other party's perspective, and find palm- palm results, can significantly impact the outgrowth of similar deals.

Assignment 9 Emotional Intelligence Navigating high- stakes accommodations can be emotionally trying. Developing emotional intelligence allows entrepreneurs to manage stress, make fellowship, and make rational opinions in grueling situations.

Assignment 10 Knowing When to Let Go While the$ 100 million offer may feel tempting, entrepreneurs must consider whether dealing their company aligns with their long- term pretensions. Knowing when to let go and move on to new gambles, or when to hold onto the business and continue growing it, is a critical decision to make.

Assignment 11 Reflecting on Success and Failure Anyhow of the outgrowth, reflecting on the trip is essential. Celebrate successes, admit failures, and use both gests to learn and grow as an entrepreneur.

Assignment 12 Giving Back Reaching inconceivable mileposts like a$ 100 million offer presents an occasion to give back to the community. Philanthropy and social responsibility can be integrated into the company's charge, making a positive impact beyond fiscal success. The trip to a $100 million offer is a transformational experience that teaches entrepreneurs precious assignments in vision, continuity, rigidity, platoon- structure, threat taking, invention, branding, client focus, concession, emotional intelligence, decision- timber, and giving back. It's not just about the plutocrat; it's about particular and professional growth, making a difference, and leaving a lasting heritage.

CHAPTER 8

Finding Purpose in Life-Altering Moments

Chancing purpose in life- altering moments can be a transformative trip that reshapes the line of one's actuality. These moments, frequently characterized by significant bouleversement, loss, or particular epiphanies, impel individualities to rethink their precedences, values, and beliefs. While grueling , they can give an occasion to discover a deeper sense of purpose and meaning in life. Life- altering moments can take colorful forms. For some, it may be the unforeseen loss of a loved one, a life hanging illness, or a major career reversal. For others, it could be a profound consummation after embarking on a soul-searching adventure, embracing a new perspective, or encountering a serendipitous event. Anyhow of the catalyst, these moments demand soul-searching and a reassessment of life's purpose. originally, these paroxysms may lead to confusion and a sense of being adrift. The familiar routines and plans that formerly handed comfort are now shattered. In similar moments, people may grapple with questions like" Why me?" or" What's the point of it all?" still, amidst the fermentation, individualities may start to uncover retired strengths, adaptability, and a renewed capacity for particular growth. The process of chancing purpose frequently involves reflecting on one's core values and beliefs. These life altering moments act as a catalyst for redefining what truly matters. It might lead someone to deflect their powers toward meaningful hobbies, connections, or causes that align with their newfound understanding of tone and the world. also, chancing purpose in similar moments may bear embracing change and letting go of once prospects. Adhering to the history or defying the present can hamper progress and help individualities from completely embracing their evolving purpose. Learning to acclimatize and accept query becomes pivotal as individualities forge a path towards meaning and fulfillment. Support systems play a vital part during these transformative times. musketeers, family, or professional counselors can give important demanded empathy, stimulant, and perspective. Engaging in open and honest exchanges with trusted individualities can help individualities gain clarity and perceptivity into their evolving sense of purpose. For some, these life-altering moments may goad them to turn their pain into a purpose- driven charge. It's not uncommon for individualities to channel their gests into enterprise that profit others. For illustration, someone who has overcome a particular struggle with dependence might devote their life to helping others on the same trip. Chancing purpose isn't always a direct process, and lapses are a natural part of the trip. It requires tolerance, tone- compassion, and an acknowledgment that the path to purpose may be marked with twists and turns. Embracing failures as openings for growth allows individualities to upgrade their sense of purpose continually. In the pursuit of purpose, awareness and tone mindfulness play pivotal places. Taking time for tone- reflection and understanding bone's heartstrings, strengths, and bournes can help individualities align their choices with their evolving sense of purpose. Practices like contemplation, journaling, or engaging in meaningful conditioning can foster tone- mindfulness and consolidate the connection to one's inner compass. Embracing vulnerability is another integral aspect of chancing purpose. It involves being authentic and embracing defects, which can lead to further profound connections with others and a lesser sense of fulfillment. By participating their gests , individualities can produce compassionate bonds that enrich their trip and support their evolving purpose. In conclusion, chancing purpose in life- altering moments is a profound and ongoing process that requires soul-searching, rigidity, and support. These moments, however frequently grueling , give an occasion for growth, tone- discovery, and the pursuit of meaning. By reflecting on core values, embracing change, and employing the power of vulnerability, individualities can transfigure adversity into purpose and produce a meaningful life path that resonates deeply with their authentic characters. The trip to purpose is noway - ending, but the prices of living a purpose- driven life are bottomless.

Beyond the Offer

In a world driven by ambition and success, opportunities are often seen as golden tickets to a better life. From job offers to educational scholarships, these opportunities hold the promise of advancement, growth, and fulfillment. However, there lies a deeper and often overlooked dimension to opportunities - what lies beyond the offer itself. This essay delves into the concept of "Beyond the Offer," aiming to unravel its meaning, significance, and the transformative potential it holds in shaping our lives and society.

Defining "Beyond the Offer"

Beyond the Offer refers to the intangible and immeasurable aspects that emerge once an opportunity is embraced. It encompasses the personal growth, learning experiences, relationships forged, and the unforeseen opportunities that arise from seizing the initial chance. It involves transcending the mere transactional nature of the offer and exploring the profound impact it has on one's character, values, and perspectives.

Beyond Material Gains

Often, opportunities are viewed through a narrow lens of material gains - a better job with a higher salary, a prestigious university degree, or a lucrative investment. However, when we look beyond these tangible benefits, we discover the immeasurable value of personal development, skill enhancement, and self-discovery that comes with pursuing these opportunities.

Embracing Challenges and Growth

Beyond the Offer lies a terrain of challenges and obstacles. It is through overcoming these hurdles that individuals grow and develop resilience. Whether it's starting a new business, taking on leadership roles, or relocating to a foreign country, these challenges test our adaptability and resourcefulness, pushing us to evolve and discover our untapped potential.

The Ripple Effect of Relationships
Opportunities often bring people together, creating networks and communities. These relationships become a catalyst for support, mentorship, and collaboration. Beyond the Offer lies the potential for lifelong friendships, inspiring mentors, and the chance to impact others positively.

Unforeseen Horizons
Beyond the Offer, serendipitous events often unfold. Unexpected connections and opportunities arise that were not part of the original plan. These unplanned experiences can lead to even greater breakthroughs, widening one's horizons beyond what was initially envisioned.

Expanding Social Impact
Beyond the Offer extends beyond the individual and reaches the realm of social impact. By leveraging opportunities, individuals can become agents of change, contributing to societal progress, and addressing pressing global issues. The ripples of these efforts can

be far-reaching and transformative, creating a cascading effect on communities and beyond.

The Pursuit of Meaning and Fulfillment
Material success alone cannot guarantee a fulfilling life. Beyond the Offer lies the pursuit of meaning and purpose, a search for a deeper sense of fulfillment. It prompts individuals to align their passions with their pursuits, seeking out opportunities that resonate with their values and aspirations.

Balancing Ambition and Well-being
In the quest for opportunities, individuals must strike a delicate balance between ambition and well-being. The pursuit of success can be all-consuming, leading to burnout and neglecting personal health and happiness. Beyond the Offer, one must also prioritize self-care, mental well-being, and nurturing meaningful relationships to lead a truly fulfilling life.

Challenges and Pitfalls
While Beyond the Offer holds immense potential, it is not without its challenges and pitfalls. The fear of failure, self-doubt, and societal pressures can hinder individuals from seizing opportunities. Moreover, the obsession with success can overshadow the essence of the journey, blinding individuals to the intrinsic value of experiences and growth.

Beyond the Offer embodies the essence of opportunities and their profound impact on individuals and society. It calls for a broader perspective that goes beyond material gains and focuses on personal growth, relationships, and the pursuit of meaning. By embracing challenges, expanding horizons, and nurturing well-being, individuals can unlock the transformative potential that lies beyond the initial offer. Only then can we truly harness the power of opportunities to shape a more purposeful and fulfilling life for ourselves and those around us.

CHAPTER 9

Continuing the Pursuit of Growth and Success

Continuing the pursuit of growth and success is a dynamic and multifaceted trip that requires fidelity, rigidity, and a growth mindset. Whether it pertains to particular development, professional trials, or any other aspect of life, seeking for nonstop enhancement is essential for achieving meaningful accomplishments and fulfillment. In this essay, I'll claw into colorful strategies and principles that can guide individualities and associations in their hunt for growth and success. Setting Clear pretensions The first step in any trip towards growth and success is defining clear and specific pretensions. pretensions give direction and provocation, serving as a roadmap for progress. Make sure your pretensions are challenging yet realistic, time-bound, and aligned with your values and heartstrings. espousing a Growth Mindset Embracing a growth mindset involves viewing challenges and lapses as openings for literacy and development. This mindset enables individualities to embrace change, take advised pitfalls, and persist in the face of adversity. nonstop literacy and Development The pursuit of growth necessitates a commitment to nonstop literacy and skill development. Stay curious and open to new knowledge, seek out instructors and experts, attend shops, and read books to expand your moxie. structure Adaptability Success frequently comes with hurdles and failures. Developing adaptability allows individualities to bounce back from lapses and maintain focus on their pretensions. Cultivate emotional intelligence, practice awareness, and foster a strong support network to enhance adaptability. Effective Time Management Time is a finite resource, so managing it wisely is pivotal. Prioritize tasks, set deadlines, and exclude distractions to optimize productivity. Consider using productivity tools and ways to make the utmost of your time. Networking and Relationship Building Success is infrequently a solitary bid. erecting a strong network of connections and connections can give precious openings, perceptivity, and support. Engage in networking events, maintain professional connections, and seek collaborations. Embracing Innovation and Creativity Embrace creativity and innovative thinking to stay ahead in a constantly evolving world. Encourage a culture of invention in associations and be open to exploring new results and ideas. Measuring and assessing Progress To continue on the path of growth, regularly assess your progress towards pretensions. Track crucial performance pointers and acclimatize your strategies as demanded. Use data- driven perceptivity to inform your opinions. Emphasizing Rigidity The pursuit of success frequently involves conforming to changing circumstances. Be willing to acclimate your plans and strategies grounded on feedback and new information. Maintaining a Positive Mindset A positive station can greatly impact your trip towards growth and success. Focus on the positive aspects of your trip, practice gratefulness, and celebrate your achievements, no matter how small. Taking Calculated pitfalls Growth and success occasionally bear stepping out of your comfort zone and taking pitfalls. Assess the implicit pitfalls and prices, make informed opinions, and be prepared for any issues. Embodying Ethical Leadership For associations, ethical leadership is vital in fostering sustainable growth and success. Lead by illustration, promote fairness, and prioritize the well- being of stakeholders. Embracing Diversity and Addition Embracing diversity and addition fosters creativity, invention, and a richer perspective. produce an inclusive terrain that values different backgrounds, ideas, and perspectives. Giving Back to the Community Contributing to the community can be a fulfilling part of the growth trip. Engage in philanthropy, levy work, or mentorship programs to make a positive impact on others' lives. Maintaining Work- Life Balance Strive for a healthy work- life balance to avoid collapse and maintain long- term success. Prioritize tone- care, relaxation, and spending time with loved bones .The pursuit of growth and success is an ongoing bid that requires a holistic approach, encompassing thing setting, literacy, adaptability, rigidity, and ethical geste . By embracing a growth mindset and fastening on nonstop enhancement, individualities and associations can thrive in their separate hobbies and leave a positive impact on the world around them. Flash back that growth and success aren't simply destinations but rather an ever- evolving trip that can be both satisfying and transformative.

CONCLUSION

In the captivating journey of "A Life-Changing Proposition: The $100M Offer Journey," readers are taken on an unforgettable expedition of self-discovery, ambition, and the power of choices. This book, authored by an enigmatic business tycoon who prefers to remain anonymous, serves as a timeless parable that navigates the realms of entrepreneurship, human relationships, and the pursuit of one's dreams. Throughout the narrative, the protagonist's relentless pursuit of a monumental $100 million offer acts as a profound metaphor, revealing deeper truths about life and the transformative impact of our decisions.

The book's central theme revolves around the transformative nature of opportunities and how they can radically alter the trajectory of one's life. As the protagonist faces the daunting challenge of securing the elusive $100 million offer, readers are presented with a myriad of lessons that resonate with universal truths. These lessons span the gamut of human emotions - from ambition and determination to fear and self-doubt. The author masterfully weaves these emotions into the tapestry of the narrative, making it relatable to every reader regardless of their background.

One of the most compelling takeaways from the book is the emphasis on embracing risk and stepping outside one's comfort zone. The protagonist's decision to embark on the $100 million offer journey is laced with uncertainties and the possibility of failure, yet it is this willingness to embrace the unknown that eventually leads to his transformation. Through this daring approach, readers are encouraged to reevaluate their own lives and contemplate the possibilities that await them if they dare to push beyond their limits.

Moreover, "A Life-Changing Proposition" demonstrates the power of resilience and perseverance. The protagonist encounters numerous setbacks and trials during his journey, each presenting an opportunity for growth and self-discovery. This resilience highlights the importance of tenacity in the face of adversity, inspiring readers to overcome their own challenges with unwavering determination.

The book also delves into the significance of personal relationships and the impact they have on our lives. As the protagonist encounters various individuals on his journey, he realizes the value of genuine connections and the ways in which they can shape our perspectives and decisions. This serves as a poignant reminder for readers to cherish the relationships they hold dear and foster meaningful connections in their own lives.

Beyond the individual journey, the narrative seamlessly transitions into exploring broader societal themes. The protagonist's pursuit of the $100 million offer involves navigating the complexities of the business world, exposing readers to the ethical dilemmas and tough decisions that entrepreneurs face. This exploration challenges readers to contemplate the role of success and wealth in society and the responsibility that accompanies it.

In conclusion, "A Life-Changing Proposition: The $100M Offer Journey" offers a powerful and transformative experience to its readers. Through a riveting narrative and a host of relatable characters, the book explores themes of ambition, risk-taking, resilience, and the value of human connections. It encourages readers to embrace opportunities, challenge their boundaries, and cultivate a deeper understanding of themselves and the world around them.

The author's masterful storytelling weaves a tale that transcends its business-focused plot, elevating it to a profound exploration of the human experience. As readers immerse themselves in the pages of this gripping narrative, they are bound to be inspired to reflect on their own lives, beliefs, and aspirations.

In the end, "A Life-Changing Proposition: The $100M Offer Journey" is not just a book but a transformative guide that implores readers to take charge of their destiny, make bold choices, and embrace the uncertainty of life. It is a testament to the potential within each of us to overcome challenges and achieve greatness, leaving an indelible mark on the hearts and minds of those who embark on this extraordinary literary odyssey.